T0153458

THE LITTLE BOOK OF

BADASS
BUSINESS

Published by OH!
20 Mortimer Street
London W1T 3JW

Disclaimer:

ISBN 978-1-91161-040-3

Editorial: Ross Hamilton,Victoria Godden
Project manager: Russell Porter
Design: Tony Seddon
Production: Jess Arvidsson

A CIP catalogue for this book is available from the British Library

Printed in Dubai

10 9 8 7 6 5 4 3 2 1

Front cover images: Matt Carr/Getty Images;
Andrew Teebay/Liverpool Echo/Mirrorpix; MediaPunch Inc/Alamy

THE LITTLE BOOK OF

BADASS
BUSINESS

CONTENTS

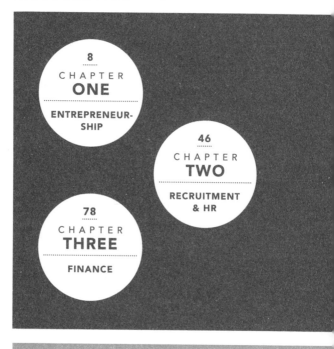

INTRODUCTION

The world of business can be a ruthless, unforgiving and even, at times, violent. It takes guts, smarts and more than a little luck to succeed in this environment, which is why sharp minds are always on the lookout for any piece of advice that could give them an edge and help them stand out from the pack.

Fortunately, you'll find dozens of such pearls of wisdom within these pages. *The Little Book of Badass Business* features more than 170 quotes from a wide variety of moguls, millionaires and titans of industry from some of the most iconic films and television series of all time. The perspectives here range from those of hard-nosed businessmen, like *Mad Men*'s Don Draper, to those whose interests are less, well, legitimate, but just as lucrative, such as *The Wire*'s Stringer Bell.

Each chapter focuses on a specific aspect of business, whether that's finding and hiring the perfect team – and keeping them in line – or controlling the message through creative marketing and savvy public relations. Perception is a powerful thing in business, after all.

From advice on building your empire from self-made men like *Breaking Bad*'s Walter White to tips on the art of negotiation from seasoned dealmakers like *The Godfather*'s Vito Corleone, this collection of bite-sized quips is essential reading for anyone looking to make their mark in the corporate, cut-throat world of business. Keep it handy, and you're sure to rise to the top… by any means necessary.

CHAPTER

1

THE BADASS
BUSINESS GUIDE TO:

ENTREPRENEURSHIP

Some of the most powerful business owners
in history started with nothing.

Find out exactly what it takes to build an empire
from the ground up – from those who've
been there and done it.

More is lost by indecision
than by wrong decision.

Tony Soprano underlines the importance
of being bold and decisive.
The Sopranos, Season 4, Episode 13: "Whitecaps"

There is gold in the streets
just waiting for someone to
come and scoop it up.

Walter White notes that there are always
opportunities if you look in the right places.
Breaking Bad, Season 5, Episode 2: "Madrigal"

In the end, we do what we have the nerve for or we disappear.

Commodore Louis Kaestner reminds us that to be successful in business, you can't lose your bottle.
Boardwalk Empire, Season 5, Episode 8: "ElDorado"

Never rat on your friends and always keep your mouth shut.

Jimmy Conway provides some essential tips for when you're first starting out in business. *Goodfellas*, 1990

I don't know if anybody's ever told you that half the time this business comes down to, 'I don't like that guy.'

Roger Sterling distils the importance of building relationships while you're building your business. *Mad Men*, Season 3, Episode 5: "The Fog"

97% of the people who quit too soon are employed by the 3% who didn't.

Jordan Belfort explains why future CEOs should never quit.
The Wolf of Wall Street, 2013

Not to be crude about it, but politics is what comes out the asshole. Wouldn't you rather be up front, feeding the horse?

Logan Roy gives a vivid analogy for why you should choose business over politics. *Succession*, Season 1, Episode 1: "Celebration"

Stop going for the easy buck and start producing something with your life. Create, instead of living off the buying and selling of others.

Carl Fox makes the case for building a business from the ground up.
Wall Street, 1987

You're born, you take shit. You get out in the world, you take more shit. You climb a little higher, you take less shit. Till one day you're up in the rarefied atmosphere and you've forgotten what shit even looks like.

Eddie Temple explains the path to success for up-and-coming entrepreneurs.
Layer Cake, 2004

In this country, you gotta make the money first. Then when you get the money, you get the power. Then when you get the power, then you get the women.

Tony Montana outlines what it means to be a success in the cut-throat world of… business.
Scarface, 1983

My point is, sometimes the answer is so obvious you can't see it because you're looking too hard.

Mike Milligan's advice, that the most obvious solution to a problem is usually the best, is invaluable when starting out in the world of business.
Fargo, Season 2, Episode 7: "Did You Do This? No, You Did It!"

You asked me if I was in the meth business, or the money business… Neither. I'm in the empire business.

Walter White shows that there's no limit to ambition when you're building a business.
Breaking Bad, Season 5, Episode 6: "Buyout"

Look the part, be the part, motherfucker.

Proposition Joe advises you to dress for the job you want, not the job you have.
The Wire, Season 1, Episode 9: "Game Day"

I don't wanna be a product of my environment. I want my environment to be a product of me.

Frank Costello demonstrates the force of will necessary to shape a company in your image.
The Departed, 2006

You have to get what you want your own way.

Tommy Shelby recommends you forge your own path on the way to commercial success.
Peaky Blinders, Season 3, Episode 6

Sometimes you gotta be willing to sacrifice your queen to win the game.

Lucious Lyon is either a keen chess player, or willing to prioritise business over everything – even family.
Empire, Season 1, Episode 9: "Unto the Breach"

There you go, finding a hidden advantage in an unfortunate circumstance; using pain to take you to the next level. Those are the things that turn players into kings.

Damon Pope congratulates those who can turn a painful situation to their advantage and profit from it.
Sons of Anarchy, Season 5, Episode 3: "Laying Pipe"

Geniuses are always branded
as crazy.

Pablo Escobar tells us that innovation in business
is often misunderstood before it becomes mainstream.
Narcos, Season 1, Episode 8: "La Gran Mentira"

Wanna trace a path to greatness? You start with defeat, loss or rejection. You want to be endlessly motivated? Failure is key.

Spencer Strasmore knows that success comes to those who have tried, failed, and keep on trying. *Ballers*, Season 5, Episode 3: "Copernicursed"

I have a competition in me. I want no one else to succeed. I hate most people.

Daniel Plainview articulates the outlook of the solo businessman who really does want to go it alone.
There Will Be Blood, 2007

Great men are not born great, they grow great.

Don Vito Corleone makes the point that no one is born to be successful. In business, you work for it.
The Godfather, 1972

All due respect, you got no fucking idea what it's like to be Number One. Every decision you make affects every facet of every other fucking thing. It's too much to deal with almost. And in the end, you're completely alone with it all.

Tony Soprano laments the responsibilities that come from being the head of your own enterprise. It's tough at the top.
The Sopranos, Season 5, Episode 13: "All Due Respect"

I don't wanna win the game.
I wanna change it.

Hakeem Lyon understands that true
entrepreneurs invent a whole new paradigm.
Empire, Season 1, Episode 5: "Dangerous Bonds"

I came to realise, it's that fear that's the worst of it. That's the real enemy. So, get up. Get out in the real world.

Walter White explains that, in business and in life, there's nothing to fear but fear itself.
Breaking Bad, Season 2, Episode 8: "Better Call Saul"

Make it simple, but significant.

Don Draper's advice applies to almost any
business idea you might have: don't overcomplicate.
Mad Men, Season 4, Episode 6: "Waldorf Stories"

Better to be lucky than to be good.

Bunk Moreland knows that no matter how hard you work, there's no better trait in business than being lucky.
The Wire, Season 4, Episode 2: "Soft Eyes"

No one gives it to you. You have to take it.

Frank Costello recommends that you never rely on getting a leg up. It's on you to make things happen.
The Departed, 2006

I'm not a traitor to my class. I am just an extreme example of what a working man can achieve.

Tommy Shelby doesn't see any issue with being a successful businessman from a working background.
Peaky Blinders, Season 4, Episode 4: "Dangerous"

Anger clouds judgement and it makes us do things that we end up regretting — things we can never take back.

David Hale advises that you make any major business decisions with a clear head.
Sons of Anarchy, Season 1, Episode 3: "Fun Town"

As the twig is bent, so grows the tree.

Pacho Herrera uses a proverb to describe how new ideas inherently push out the old ones.
Narcos, Season 1, Episode 9: "La Catedral"

A man who only talks business is a failure in all aspects of life.

Camino Del Rio is of the opinion that business cannot overcome all other aspects of life — there needs to be a balance.

Ozark, Season 1, Episode 8: "Kaleidoscope"

Ordinary men avoid trouble. Extraordinary men turn it to their advantage.

Gaston Means knows that true entrepreneurs shine in adversity.
Boardwalk Empire, Season 3, Episode 2: "Spaghetti and Coffee"

This is America. Pick a job and become the person who does it.

Bobbie Barrett's advice on getting started is also useful for those of you outside the USA.
Mad Men, Season 2, Episode 5: "The New Girl"

The only thing standing between you and your goal is the bullshit story you keep telling yourself as to why you can't achieve it.

Jordan Belfort has some hard truths for aspiring businesspeople with too many excuses.
The Wolf of Wall Street, 2013

You know what capitalism is?
Getting fucked!

Tony Montana articulates the intricacies of the
modern business environment.
Scarface, 1983

It's good to be in something from the ground floor. I came too late for that, and I know. But lately I'm getting the feeling that I came in at the end. The best is over.

Tony Soprano sings the praises of investing early in a project — and not letting it outstay its welcome.
The Sopranos, Season 1, Episode 1: "Pilot"

CHAPTER

2

RECRUITMENT & HR

They say that a boss is only as good as
the people they employ, so why settle for
anything less than the best?

These quotes from badass business leaders
demonstrate how to find and hire the perfect
team – and how to keep them in line.

The best way to bond with someone isn't doing a favour, it's asking for one.

Chuck Rhoades knows that the quickest way to build rapport is showing someone you value their skills.
Billions, Season 2, Episode 4: "The Oath"

Middle management means that you got just enough responsibility to listen when people talk, but not so much you can't tell anybody to go fuck themselves.

Major Howard "Bunny" Colvin on the benefits of having just a little authority.
The Wire, Season 3, Episode 5: "Straight and True"

You don't shit where you eat.
And you really don't shit where
I eat.

Tony Soprano warns against mixing business
with pleasure.
The Sopranos, Season 6, Episode 7: "Luxury Lounge"

If you're soft on rebellion, it'll grow.

Tommy Shelby warns that you can't allow
dissent in the boardroom to go unpunished.
Peaky Blinders, Season 3, Episode 2

My father taught me many things here. He taught me in this room. He taught me: keep your friends close, but your enemies closer.

Michael Corleone passes on some family wisdom: sometimes it's better to bring your enemies in-house.
The Godfather Part II, 1974

Honourable men go with honourable men.

Giovanni Cappa explains that if you act right, you'll attract the right personnel. The same goes for women too.
Mean Streets, 1973

Well, I've got to learn a lot of peoples' names before I fire them.

Roger Sterling shows how to deal tactfully with unfortunate redundancies.
Mad Men, Season 4, Episode 12: "Blowing Smoke"

Give them to me young, hungry and stupid. And in no time, I will make them rich.

Jordan Belfort outlines his three most desirable traits in an employee.
The Wolf of Wall Street, 2013

That's the problem with a family business. Now, if one of my men defies me, puts a deal in jeopardy, I take his arm. If he talks out of turn, I take his tongue. But you, your children, your grandchildren… what are you willing to do to show us you're committed?

Joe Bulo highlights the problems of going into business with your family.
Fargo, Season 2, Episode 4: "Fear and Trembling"

When they say they're more than a little concerned, they're desperate.

Frank Sheeran translates the language of the modern human resources manager.
The Irishman, 2019

Success. It's got enemies. You can be successful and have enemies or you can be unsuccessful and have friends.

Dominic Cattano opines that if you haven't made some enemies in the workplace, you haven't made it.
American Gangster, 2007

The key to this business is personal relationships.

Dickie Fox reminds us that building a connection
with your associates can unlock all sorts of opportunities.
Jerry Maguire, 1996

I don't lie to myself and I don't hold on to a loser.

Bobby "Axe" Axelrod explains that there's no room for sentimentality when dealing with underperforming employees.
Billions, Season 1, Episode 4: "Short Squeeze"

Nobody works with me. People work for me.

Billy Kimber's attitude will strike a chord with anyone who's not willing to share executive responsibilities.
Peaky Blinders, Season 1, Episode 2

It ain't easy being king.

Jax Teller laments the difficulties of the CEO life.
Sons of Anarchy, Season 1, Episode 1: "Pilot"

Fuck pride. Pride only hurts,
it never helps.

Marsellus Wallace warns against missing out on
potentially lucrative opportunities because of
misplaced pride.
Pulp Fiction, 1994

Some people are immune to good advice.

Saul Goodman knows that there's no helping some stubborn proteges, so cut them loose.
Breaking Bad, Season 5, Episode 11: "Confessions"

My cholesterol is high enough. Don't butter my ass — just get smarter.

Bobby "Axe" Axelrod is a proponent of straight talking in the workplace.
Billions, Season 1, Episode 1: "Pilot"

I'm gonna show you as gently as I can how much you don't know.

Dennis "Cutty" Wise demonstrates the diplomatic way to tell a colleague that they're full of it.
The Wire, Season 4, Episode 4: "Refugees"

If you can quote the rules,
then you can fucking obey
them, do you understand?

Tony Soprano has a gentle reminder for any
employees taking liberties with the company handbook.
The Sopranos, Season 4, Episode 9: "Whoever Did This"

Human beings, you see, have no inherent value other than the money they earn. Cats have value, for example, because they provide pleasure to the humans. But a deadbeat on welfare? Well, they have negative value.

V. M. Varga epitomises the more transactional side to human resources.
Fargo, Season 3, Episode 10: "Somebody to Love"

The streets aren't made for everybody. That's why they made sidewalks.

Cookie Lyon knows that not everybody has what it takes to put in the work and grind.
Empire, Season 1, Episode 2: "The Outspoken King"

When I ask somebody to take care of something for me, I expect them to take care of it themselves. I don't need two roads coming back to me.

Russell Bufalino doesn't expect the tasks he delegates to be delegated.
The Irishman, 2019

Nothing governs like fear.

James "Ghost" St. Patrick prefers to be feared rather than loved when it comes to keeping his team on track.
Power, Season 4, Episode 8: "It's Done"

To make sure your dog obeys you, you have to show it the stick once in a while.

C.I. Chester Campbell is more an advocate of the "stick" than the "carrot" when it comes to employee motivation.
Peaky Blinders, Season 2, Episode 5

Foolishness is right next door to strength.

Wendy Rhoades reminds you to look closely at your candidates when hiring.
Billions, Season 2, Episode 11: "Golden Frog Time"

We're building something here, detective, we're building it from scratch. All the pieces matter.

Lester Freamon reminds us that every hire is important when building your company.
The Wire, Season 1, Episode 6: "The Wire"

Buck, if I wanted an opinion from an asshole, I'd ask my own. Got it?

Ray Stussy demonstrates one way of moderating a brainstorm meeting.
Fargo, Season 3, Episode 4: "The Narrow Escape Problem"

I don't want to hear about none of you tomorrow morning on *TMZ*, *Deadspin* or Page fucking Six. Do not fuck up. I repeat, do not fuck up.

Spencer Strasmore drives home the importance of not sullying your employer's reputation through your own actions.
Ballers, Season 1, Episode 3: "Move the Chains"

I can promise you that I am spiritually and emotionally and ethically and morally behind whoever wins.

Stewy Hosseini knows that when an outcome is uncertain, it pays to keep your options open.
Succession, Season 1, Episode 6: "Whose Side Are You On?

CHAPTER

3

FINANCE

Money may not buy you happiness, but it will
keep you in business.

Read these green-tinted quotes
if you ever need a reminder to always keep
your eye on the bottom line.

Man, money ain't got no owners.
Only spenders.

Omar Little warns that having capital is never
a permanent state of affairs.
The Wire, Season 4, Episode 4: "Refugees"

Would you like to hear my favourite passage from Shakespeare? Take the fucking money.

Logan Roy shares some business wisdom from the Bard. Probably.
Succession, Season 2, Episode 5: "Tern Haven"

Don't be immoral with the money, do what's right, you understand?

Jimmy Conway reminds us that money comes
with certain responsibilities (though your definition
of immorality may vary).
Goodfellas, 1990

Just cash the cheques, you're going to die one day.

Ted Chaough's financial philosophy is: spend it while you can.
Mad Men, Season 7, Episode 2: "A Day's Work"

Let me tell you something.
There's no nobility in poverty.
I've been a rich man and I've
been a poor man. And I choose
rich every fucking time.

Jordan Belfort dispels the myth that money can't
buy you happiness.
The Wolf of Wall Street, 2013

Greed, for lack of a better word, is good. Greed is right, greed works. Greed clarifies, cuts through, and captures the essence of the evolutionary spirit.

Gordon Gekko outlines the virtues of avarice when it comes to cold, hard cash.
Wall Street, 1987

Money is not peace of mind. Money is not happiness. Money is, at its essence, that measure of a man's choices.

Marty Byrde makes it clear that you shouldn't expect money to solve all your problems. You have to use it in the right way.
Ozark, Season 1, Episode 1: "Sugarwood"

Show me the money!

Rod Tidwell does what any astute businessman should and asks to see the cash.
Jerry Maguire, 1996

Anybody who tells you money is the root of all evil doesn't fucking have any.

Jim Young explains why you shouldn't worry about the moral implications of your bank balance.
Boiler Room, 2000

When you've run out of ways to hide your money, that's when you give it to the poor.

Steve Murphy explains how some businessmen come to be seen as philanthropists.
Narcos, Season 1, Episode 2: "The Sword of Simón Bolívar"

Money is not beside the point…
Money is the point.

Jimmy McGill aims to make sure you remember the
ultimate goal in business.
Better Call Saul, Season 1, Episode 1: "Uno"

Here's my first bit of financial advice. Don't invest in depreciating assets. If it drives, flies, floats or fucks, lease it.

Spencer Strasmore has some essential advice for anyone building up their portfolio.
Ballers, Season 1, Episode 1: "Pilot"

A fool and his money are lucky enough to get together in the first place.

Gordon Gekko has no sympathy for folks who lose it all through bad investments.
Wall Street, 1987

What's the point of having 'fuck you money' if you never say fuck you.

Bobby "Axe" Axelrod knows that being rich means you don't have to be humble.
Billions, Season 1, Episode 1: "Pilot"

You sentimentalise property, you can kiss profits goodbye.

Marty Byrde reminds you not to get attached to
your assets unless you want your bottom line to suffer.
Ozark, Season 1, Episode 4: "Tonight We Improvise"

Fuck 'right'. It ain't about right, it's about money.

D'Angelo Barksdale explains that financial success doesn't always sit kindly with morality.
The Wire, Season 1, Episode 2: "Refugees"

What's worth doing is worth doing for money.

Gordon Gekko reminds you to never offer your
services for free.
Wall Street, 1987

Buy land… 'cause God ain't making any more of it.

Tony Soprano has some sound investment advice for anyone looking to broaden their portfolio. *The Sopranos*, Season 4, Episode 7: "Watching Too Much Television"

Remember. Richest guy in the room is always the boss.

Nikki Swango postulates that titles don't matter
when it comes to seniority — money talks.
Fargo, Season 3, Episode 4: "The Narrow Escape Problem"

You're not a saint. Saints don't live on Park Avenue.

Cynthia Baum makes the observation that you don't buy a Manhattan penthouse without fleecing a few people.
The Big Short, 2015

Everything caves under the weight of greed. I've seen it my whole life. Nothing stays simple. **99**

Elliott Oswald warns not to let your desire for money outstrip your company's ability to generate it.
Sons of Anarchy, Season 2, Episode 7: "Gilead"

Look, I am not a rich person. I am a poor person with money.

Pablo Escobar outlines the different perspective you gain as a person who's worked their way up from nothing. *Narcos*, Season 1, Episode 3: "The Men of Always"

You see, the hard reality is how much money we accumulate in life is not a function of who's president or the economy or bubbles bursting or bad breaks or bosses.

Marty Byrde is a believer that your balance sheet is a reflection of you alone — everything else is just an excuse. *Ozark*, Season 1, Episode 1: "Sugarwood"

Here's the thing about being rich, okay? It's fucking great. It's like being a superhero, only better. You get to do what you want, the authorities can't really touch you. You get to wear a costume, but it's designed by Armani and it doesn't make you look like a prick.

Tom Wambsgans waxes lyrical about the perks of being in the executive class.
Succession, Season 1, Episode 6: "Whose Side Are You On?"

Money's only something
you need in case you don't
die tomorrow.

Carl Fox explains the limits to cashing a huge
bonus cheque.
Wall Street, 1987

Work until your bank account
looks like a phone number.

Jordan Belfort recommends you don't stop until
there are at least two commas in your bank balance.
The Wolf of Wall Street, 2013

'Remember when' is the lowest form of conversation.

Tony Soprano knows that past performance is no guarantee of future success, so be wary when making investments.
The Sopranos, Season 6, Episode 15: "Remember When"

I love money more than
the things it can buy… but what
I love more than money is
other people's money.

Jordan Belfort recommends you don't stop until
there are at least two commas in your bank balance.
The Wolf of Wall Street, 2013

CHAPTER

4

THE BADASS BUSINESS GUIDE TO:

MARKETING & PR

Perception is a powerful thing in business, as these quotes from badass tycoons show.

Make sure that you're always controlling the message, whether it's going to your friends, the public, or your enemies…

My name is my name.

Marlo Stanfield underlines that, ultimately,
reputation is everything.
The Wire, Season 5, Episode 9: "Late Editions"

If you're committed enough, you can make any story work. I once told a woman I was Kevin Costner and it worked because I believed it.

Saul Goodman knows the key to a great sales pitch is complete commitment.
Breaking Bad, Season 3, Episode 11: "Abiquiu"

If you don't like what's being said, change the conversation. **99**

Don Draper knows that it's essential to control
the narrative in business.
Mad Men, Season 3, Episode 2: "Love Among the Ruins"

The loudest one in the room is the weakest one in the room.

Frank Lucas recommends a more subtle approach to marketing.
American Gangster, 2007

Got to look successful to
be successful.

Jimmy McGill subscribes to the "dress to
impress" business doctrine.
Better Call Saul, Season 1, Episode 7: "Bingo"

Yeah now, well, the thing about the old days... they the old days.

Slim Charles knows that nostalgia can be a powerful marketing tool, but you shouldn't forget that the past is the past.
The Wire, Season 4, Episode 3: "Home Rooms"

Those who want respect, give respect.

Tony Soprano explains you reap what you sow when it comes to your company's image.
The Sopranos, Season 2, Episode 12: "The Knight in White Satin Armor"

There's no magic formula for what it is we do. All financial firms are more or less the same, I'm not gonna lie to you. But what separates us is the work we put in, all phases of the game.

Joe Krutel admits that there's no substitute for hard work when it comes to winning over clients. *Ballers*, Season 1, Episode 4: "Heads Will Roll"

One's eyes can be deceived.
We see what we believe,
not the other way around.

V. M. Varga shows that you can cultivate a healthy
image for your company by giving people what they want.
Fargo, Season 3, Episode 10: "Somebody to love"

Lies are necessary, when the truth
is too difficult to believe.

Pablo Escobar explains that there are occasions when
"creative" publicity is preferable to the literal variety.
Narcos, Season 1, Episode 8: "La Gran Mentira"

This here game is more than the rep you carry, the corner you hold. You gotta be fierce, I know that, but more than that, you gotta show some flex, give and take on both sides.

Stringer Bell knows that a tough image will only get you so far — you need to be open to compromise.
The Wire, Season 2, Episode 9: "Stray Rounds"

People want to be told what to do so badly that they'll listen to anyone.

Don Draper gets at the essential need for direction that people have — just make sure you're the one telling them.

Mad Men, Season 1, Episode 6: "Babylon"

The bigger the lie, the more they believe.

Bunk Moreland shows that the more liberal you are with your advertising, the easier it is for folks to accept. *The Wire*, Season 3, Episode 7: "Back Burners"

Truth is like poetry. And most people fucking hate poetry.

Overheard in a bar, this piece of wisdom shows that sometimes it's better to offer an "alternative" view of events to the public.
The Big Short, 2015

Conscience do cost.

"Mostly Blind" Butchie explains that operating
ethically has a price, even if it's the right thing to do.
The Wire, Season 3, Episode 7: "Back Burners"

Best way to make a bad story go away is to come up with a better story, and sell it hard.

Steve Murphy reveals the number one way for your PR team to conduct damage control.
Narcos, Season 2, Episode 9: "Nuestra Finca"

People deserve a second chance, just like businesses.

Marty Byrde advocates that nobody, and no company, should be cancelled because of a single mistake.
Ozark, Season 1, Episode 3: "My Dripping Sleep"

It wasn't a lie, it was ineptitude with insufficient cover.

Don Draper's line covers just about any potential untruth your company may end up peddling.
Mad Men, Season 1, Episode 3: "Marriage of Figaro"

At some point, the only way to succeed is to not give a fuck.

Spencer Strasmore thinks that, ultimately, the only opinion that counts is your own.
Ballers, Season 5, Episode 4: "Municipal"

Conscience gets expensive, doesn't it?

Saul Goodman knows that there's a price to be
paid for keeping clean in the eyes of the public.
Breaking Bad, Season 2, Episode 9: "Better Call Saul"

If anybody asks you if you in this game, you tell 'em you in it for life, a'ight?

D'Angelo Barksdale wants to ensure that the public line is always positive, even if things aren't good behind the scenes.
The Wire, Season 1, Episode 12: "Cleaning Up"

If you smell smoke, it's because there's a fire. So you're going to have to stamp that out quickly.

Rosalind Pearson recommends you address even minor issues before they have the chance to become PR disasters.
The Gentlemen, 2019

CHAPTER

5

THE BADASS
BUSINESS GUIDE TO:

NEGOTIATION

Sometimes, you need to make a deal.

But that doesn't mean you can't still
get exactly what you want, as these quotes
from hard-nosed negotiators show.

Whisky's good proofing water.
Tells you who's real and
who isn't.

Tommy Shelby makes the case for keeping a
liquor cabinet in your boardroom.
Peaky Blinders, Season 1, Episode 3

This was supposed to be choreographed. That's about as choreographed as a dog getting fucked on roller skates.

Logan Roy explains how *not* to go about purchasing your rival's company.
Succession, Season 2, Episode 3: "Hunting"

A friend should always underestimate your virtues and an enemy overestimate your faults.

Vito Corleone explains that how you're perceived can skew any deal in your favour.
The Godfather, 1972

You should never underestimate the predictability of stupidity.

Bullet Tooth Tony reminds us that, sometimes, it's best not to overthink your opposition at the negotiating table.
Snatch, 2000

It's business. Leave your emotions at the door.

Jordan Belfort's advice for negotiating:
nothing's personal.
The Wolf of Wall Street, 2013

A-B-C. A-Always, B-Be, C-Closing. Always be closing.

Blake breaks down the art of sales into three elemental words.
Glengarry Glen Ross, 1992

A sale is made on every call you make. Either you sell the client some stock or he sells you a reason he can't. Either way a sale is made, the only question is who is gonna close?

Jim Young explains that every interaction you have with a potential customer is transactional. *Boiler Room*, 2000

I'm gonna make him an offer he can't refuse.

Vito Corleone is a firm believer that everybody
has their price.
The Godfather, 1972

The only way to guarantee peace
is by making the prospect of
war seem hopeless.

Tommy Shelby shows that you can negotiate your
desired outcome by making other results untenable.
Peaky Blinders, Season 3, Episode 2

When I pull a deal off the table, I leave Nagasaki behind.

Bobby "Axe" Axelrod shows that if you're not getting anywhere, sometimes it's best to blow the deal up. *Billions*, Season 1, Episode 12: "The Conversation"

No deal, no dice. Shot at and
missed. Shit on and hit.

Saul Goodman uses the gift of the gab to bat
away derisory offers.
Breaking Bad, Season 2, Episode 11: "Mandala"

Lambs go to slaughter. A man,
he learns when to walk away.

The Greek reminds you not to be a sheep
when chasing your next payday.
The Wire, Season 2, Episode 12: "Port In a Storm"

A deal is always better than war.

Floyd Gerhardt would rather avoid collateral damage when negotiating.
Fargo, Season 2, Episode 4: "Fear and Trembling"

A guy told me one time… don't let yourself get attached to anything you are not willing to walk out on in 30 seconds flat if you feel the heat around the corner.

Neil McCauley insists that you always need to be willing to walk away from a deal if circumstances change. *Heat*, 1995

We're going to wait and we're going to wait and we're going to wait until they feel the pain. Until they start to bleed.

Mark Baum prefers to let the pressure build
and build to really create leverage in a negotiation.
The Big Short, 2015

An agreement is not the same thing as an assurance.

C.I. Chester Campbell recommends that even when a deal is done, you don't take the outcome for granted.
Peaky Blinders, Season 2, Episode 5

Fair's for losers. I'd rather win.

A.J. Weston doesn't think you should worry about cutting a fair deal – as long as you're on the right side of it.
Sons of Anarchy, Season 2, Episode 12: "The Culling"

When you kill someone, you lose all your leverage the moment they're dead. Now, you take someone's children away from them, you'd be amazed what they'd do to get them back.

Steve Murphy's extreme example demonstrates just how important gaining leverage is in negotiating. *Narcos*, Season 1, Episode 7: "You Will Cry Tears of Blood"

We got a deal, but just so we're clear, my ice box is filled with pieces of fellas who tried to fuck me over.

Manny Horvitz offers an excellent line to use the next time you conclude a negotiation. *Boardwalk Empire*, Season 2, Episode 9: "Battle of the Century"

You don't parley when you're on the back foot.

Tommy Shelby is adamant that you should only offer terms from a position of strength.
Peaky Blinders, Season 1, Episode 2

Sometimes it is a big dick competition.

Kendall Roy believes that occasionally a deal really does boil down to anatomy.
Succession, Season 1, Episode 1: "Celebration"

> **Luca Brasi held a gun to his head, and my father assured him that either his brains or his signature would be on the contract.**

Michael Corleone describes a fool-proof technique to gain that elusive signature.
The Godfather, 1972

Only one thing counts in this world: Get them to sign on the line which is dotted.

Blake sets out the single most important outcome of any business deal: the signature.
Glengarry Glen Ross, 1992

A wise man does not burn his bridges until he first knows he can part the waters.

Norman Wilson espouses the benefits of keeping all your options open in a negotiation.
The Wire, Season 4, Episode 11: "A New Day"

Rum's for fun and fucking, innit? So, whisky, now that… that is for business.

Alfie Solomons outlines the difference between corporate and recreational spirits.
Peaky Blinders, Season 2, Episode 2

There's only one rule in this jungle. When the lion is hungry, he eats.

Mickey Pearson likes to remind adversaries that he abides by a simple code.
The Gentlemen, 2019

CHAPTER

6

TAKING ON THE COMPETITION

The world of business is a cut-throat one.

Use these quotes as motivation for outmanoeuvring your rivals and crushing your enemies – by whatever means necessary.

Come at the king, you best not miss.

Omar Little offers some words of warning in the face of a hostile takeover.
The Wire, Season 1, Episode 8: "Lessons"

Revenge is a dish best served cold.

Vito Corleone preaches patience. Don't rush to hit back at your rivals — make them wait.
The Godfather, 1972

A good matador doesn't try to kill a fresh bull. You wait until he's been stuck a few times.

Chuck Rhoades preaches patience before going in for the kill.
Billions, Season 1, Episode 1: "Pilot"

Sun-tzu: If your enemy is superior, evade him. If angry, irritate him. If equally matched, fight, and if not split and reevaluate.

Bud Fox paraphrases *The Art of War*, which can be just as valuable in the world of business.
Wall Street, 1987

I like hurting human beings as much as the next guy, but this is really fucking good.

Roman Roy takes more pleasure than is perhaps advisable in taking down his rivals.
Succession, Season 1, Episode 8: "Prague"

There's no such thing as too far. You understand? You push everything as far as you can. You push and you push and you push until it starts pushing back. And then you push some goddamn more.

Walter Abrams demonstrates the relentless attitude you need to beat out your rivals.
Two for the Money, 2005

Don't underestimate the other guy's greed.

Frank Lopez's words of wisdom are always valuable when sizing up your opposition.
Scarface, 1983

Impose your will on him until he does what he needs to and repays the debt.

Wendy Rhoades says that sheer force of will can be enough to secure your desired outcome.
Billions, Season 3, Episode 2: "The Wrong Maria Gonzalez"

Just because you shot Jesse James, don't make you Jesse James.

Mike Ehrmantraut reminds us that the work doesn't end with overcoming your competition. *Breaking Bad*, Season 5, Episode 3: "Hazard Pay"

The thing about war is, it's just bad for business. And when you got a bull's-eye on your back, your rivals get bold.

Steve Murphy explains that when you're a target, it can make your business vulnerable.
Narcos, Season 1, Episode 7: "You Will Cry Tears of Blood"

If the gods are fucking you, you find a way to fuck them back.

Ervin Burrell expects you to take no shit if you're having business troubles — even from the almighty.
The Wire, Season 3, Episode 1: "Time After Time"

We're soldiers. Soldiers don't go to hell. It's war. Soldiers kill other soldiers. We're in a situation where everyone involved knows the stakes and if you are going to accept those stakes, you've got to do certain things. It's business.

Tony Soprano shows that even in the most brutal of business dealings, it's nothing personal.
The Sopranos, Season 2, Episode 9: "From Where to Eternity"

At some level, food knows
it's food.

V. M. Varga explains that, in the world of business,
there is an inherent hierarchy.
Fargo, Season 3, Episode 9: "Aporia"

The game is out there, and it's either play or get played.

Omar Little distils the dog-eat-dog nature of "the game".
The Wire, Season 1, Episode 8: "Lessons"

You don't have to outswim the shark.
You just have to outswim the
guy you're scuba diving with.

Orrin Bach brings the nature of competition into
sharp relief.
Billions, Season 1, Episode 1: "Pilot"

It's like one of those nature shows. You mess with the environment, some species get fucked out of their habitat.

Thomas "Herc" Hauk outlines how disrupting the marketplace can push smaller, independent businesses out.
The Wire, Season 3, Episode 7: "Back Burners"

The purpose of war is peace.

Pablo Escobar reminds us that conflict in business is a means, not an end.
Narcos, Season 1, Episode 9: "La Catedral"

People hate to think about bad things happening so they always underestimate their likelihood.

Jamie Shipley shows you how you can see opportunities other businesspeople miss by being just a little pessimistic.
The Big Short, 2015

Rule one, you don't punch above your weight.

Polly Gray advises that you don't pick a fight that you can't win.
Peaky Blinders, Season 1, Episode 2

The moral of the story is I chose a half measure when I should have gone all the way. I'll never make that mistake again.

Mike Ehrmantraut learns a valuable lesson —
make sure your rivals are dead and buried.
Breaking Bad, Season 3, Episode 12: "Half Measures"

The shallow end of the pool is
where the turds float.

V. M. Varga recommends that you don't concern
yourself with trivial matters, and go straight for the
big guns — the "deep end", if you like.
Fargo, Season 3, Episode 6: "The Lord of No Mercy"

You strike when your enemy is weak.

Tommy Shelby echoes the classic wisdom that your best chance of taking out a competitor is when they're at their lowest.

Peaky Blinders, Season 1, Episode 2

Don't matter who did what to who at this point. Fact is, we went to war and now there ain't no goin' back. I mean, shit, it's what war is, you know? Once you in it, you in it. If it's a lie, then we fight on that lie. But we gotta fight.

Slim Charles explains that conflict can often be a point of principle. Sometimes, business acumen doesn't come into it.
The Wire, Season 3, Episode 12: "Mission Accomplished"

Don't go setting fires where there's nothing to burn.

Clay Morrow warns against pursuing lost causes that can spread your company too thin.
Sons of Anarchy, Season 4, Episode 2: "Booster"

You want it to be one way.
But it's the other way.

Marlo Stanfield delivers a simple but devastating
statement for when you've taken control of a situation. Try it
next time you're facing off across the boardroom table.
The Wire, Season 4, Episode 4: "Refugees"

There is a time to fight and there is a time to be clever.

Pablo Escobar knows that sometimes outward conflict isn't the smartest move for you or your company. *Narcos*, Season 1, Episode 10: "Despegue"

I drink your milkshake.
I drink it up.

Daniel Plainview uses a theatrical flourish to
communicate that "what's yours is mine".
There Will Be Blood, 2007

The most valuable commodity
I know of is information.

Gordon Gekko subscribes to the "knowledge is
power" school of business.
Wall Street, 1987

You gotta start thinking about this.
The position you're in now,
you become a target.

Spencer Strasmore warns that the more successful
you are, the more people will try to take it from you.
Ballers, Season 1, Episode 5: "Machete Charge"

The game is rigged, but you cannot lose if you do not play.

Marla Daniels makes the point that your competitors can't beat you if you refuse to play by their rules. Make your own.
The Wire, Season 1, Episode 2: "The Detail"

Your problem is you spent your whole life thinking there are rules. There aren't.

Lorne Malvo cuts to the chase and tells us that if you want to get ahead, then don't play by the rules.
Fargo, Season 1, Episode 1: "The Crocodile's Dilemma"